The Ohio
Reader

By Marcia Schonberg

Illustrated by K.L. Darnell

Sleeping Bear Press™

310 North Main Street, Suite 300
Chelsea, MI 48118
www.sleepingbearpress.com

THOMSON

*──── ™

GALE

© 2007 Thomson Gale, a part of the Thomson Corporation.

Thomson, Star Logo and Sleeping Bear Press are trademarks
and Gale is a registered trademark used herein under license.

Printed and bound in China.

10 9 8 7 6 5 4 3 2 1

Library of Congress Cataloging-in-Publication Data.

Schonberg, Marcia.
The Ohio reader / written by Marcia Schonberg ; illustrated by K.L. Darnell.
p. cm. — (State reader series)
Summary: "Modeled after traditional primers, this book includes individual stories, riddles,
and poems about Ohio's history, famous people, and state symbols"—Provided by publisher.
ISBN 10: 1-58536-321-9
ISBN 13: 978-1-58536-321-6
1. Ohio—Literary collections. 2. Ohio—Juvenile literature. I. Darnell, Kathryn. II. Title.
PS3619.C4537O38 2007
818′.60809771   2007005485

Preface

True stories, one about a brave young Ohioan another telling how a former slave shared his wealth with his community, and many others fill the pages of this reader. They are but a few of the intriguing tales I discovered through years of Ohio research. A narrative poem relies on memories from my own children's childhood. Another entry journals days of my summer vacations spent along the Lake Erie shore when I was young. The list continues as I share my Ohio connection through short stories, poems, games, and riddles.

The content of *The Ohio Reader* crosses many ages and grade levels, just as the original *McGuffey Readers* written in Ohio by educator William McGuffey did during the 1800s. The content also spans the history of Ohio, from early statehood to current times. I've tucked in timelines and facts, but also a tip of my hat toward the merit of virtues—that lead toward living in harmony within our homes, schools, communities, and world.

My hope is to help increase literacy and improve reading skills while providing useful and entertaining information. I hope you, parents, teachers, and young readers, will enjoy sharing these pages. Let them spark your creativity. I encourage you to create activities and projects based on *The Ohio Reader*. Have fun!

Best wishes for sunny days and bright ideas,
Marcia Schonberg

These stories are for my young Ohio readers—ones I've met or hope to meet! And to Bill, Adam, David, Lisa, Jeff, Joey, and Brandon for all the stories we share.

MARCIA

For Marge & Jim Mitts.

KATE

Table of Contents

An Ohio Pledge
by Marcia Schonberg

I love to travel far and wide
And learn where 'er I roam
But I'm a Buckeye through and through—
Ohio is my home.

I know about her cities
And her counties, 88.
And I'm happy when I say,
"Ohio's really great!"

*Ohio has another state pledge, "I salute the flag of the state
of Ohio and pledge to the Buckeye State respect and loyalty."
It was adopted in 2002 by Ohio legislators to honor the 200th
birthday of the Ohio flag. You can say this pledge after reciting
the national Pledge of Allegiance.*

Who Am I?
Animal Riddles

I live in the woods.
And play in the park.
I sit up tall
To eat nuts hiding in the leaves.
I store some for winter
And swish my bushy tail.

I pick up seeds with my sharp beak
And fly from tree to tree.
I can sing, but I cannot talk.
A pointy crest sits atop my head.
My feathers, the color of holly berries,
Gleam against the snow.

My big teeth chop
Thick branches, sticks, and twigs
To build my cozy house.
My brown fur stays dry
Even when I swim.
And my house—is a river dam.

My soft brown fur and antlers tall
Do not hide me very well
From hunters in the fall.
But other times, with hikers near,
I swiftly run away in fear
Although they mean no harm.

Marblehead Lighthouse

Walk carefully along the rocks.
Climb old lighthouse steps with me.
Up and up, round and round—
Remember how it used to be?

When Rachel Wolcott stood at the peak
Sending a beam so bright,
Keeping ships far off the shore
From crashing in the night?

Leave our picnic lunch below
And climb the lighthouse steps with me.
Up and up, round and round—
How far can you see?

While Marblehead is fast asleep
The beacon flashes green
Warning ships far off the shore
Of dangers that can't be seen.

With one hand she grabbed the many layers of skirts that hung around her ankles to keep herself from tripping on them. In her other hand Rachel carried the heavy whale oil. Rachel Wolcott trudged round and round, up and up until she reached the top.

Lake Erie captains were counting on her to reach the top of the Marblehead Light in time to kindle the oil lamps. Ever since her husband, Benajah, died of cholera Rachel climbed the limestone steps each day.

She and Benajah came to Ohio from Connecticut after the Revolutionary War. Her husband, claiming a small piece of the Western Reserve, became the first keeper of Marblehead Lighthouse and among the pioneer town's earliest settlers.

Now, in 1832, Rachel set out from her small stone house to tend the tall lighthouse, about three miles away. As the first female lighthouse keeper on the Great Lakes, Rachel tracked weather conditions and sent rescuers when ships, boats, or freighters needed help. She kept a log of the ships that passed by the lighthouse on the tip of Marblehead Peninsula. Her hardest job, carrying the whale oil, kept the 13 lights burning throughout the night. The lamps warned sailors of Lake Erie's dangerous and rocky shoals.

Rachel kept up her daily job at the lighthouse for two years. Then she married Jeremiah van Benschoten. He became the third keeper.

This cone-shaped lighthouse first shed its beacon over Sandusky Bay in 1822. It is the oldest lighthouse in continuous operation on the Great Lakes. Marblehead Lighthouse operates electrically now, without the need for a lighthouse keeper. The United States Coast Guard watches over the lighthouse. The lighthouse watches over Lake Erie by flashing a green signal every 11 seconds.

Apple Trees
A nature poem

When I was little
My parents planted three tiny apple trees.
One for my brother, one for my sister,
And one to honor me.

We watered them and wondered when
They would ever grow
Big enough to cast the shade
Or blossom in a row.

As we grew, we long forgot
To tend those apple trees.
But every year they bloom in spring
As if to say, "Come back and you will see..."

Apples green, and red
And golden in the fall.
Bushels full for siblings three
And shade for one and all.

Grandma's Kitchen

Grandma's kitchen sparkles. She loves to spend time there, cooking and baking for her family. "It's my favorite room," she says. She has all the latest equipment and every gadget you can think of. Cold water and ice cubes seem to magically come from the fridge door. Her convection oven and microwave speed up cooking. Her Crock-Pot slows down cooking. Four fancy stools stand at attention along the counter. I like to sit and chat there, keeping her company while she cooks.

One of her specialties, at least to me and my cousins, is her delicious applesauce.

Making applesauce with her is one of my favorite projects. First, she asks me to help her pick apples at the orchard. We pick Cortlands and Empire apples off the low branches. They are red with specks of green and yellow showing through. "These will cook into the most delicious shade of pink you've ever seen—or tasted!" Grandma promises. We wash them and cut them into quarters. When the bowl is piled high, we splash a little apple cider over them and cover the bowl with plastic wrap.

She places the apple bowl in the microwave and I press the cook button. When the sweet smell of cooked apples fills the kitchen, Grandma opens the door. She carefully pokes the apples with a fork. They are done when they slide off, she says. I say they are finished when they are soft, mushy, and shrink deep into the bowl. We are both amazed. "It takes so little time with the modern convenience of a microwave," she says.

Now for the old-fashioned part: Grandma takes out her food mill. It has little holes like a colander and a shiny metal handle that turns like a crank, pushing the cooked apples through. "I've been using this old-fashioned contraption for more than 40 years," she says. "My mother gave it to me when Grandpa and I got married—it's just like the one she had. She and I used to make applesauce. Making applesauce with you reminds me of those days," Grandma says as she smiles.

We place the food mill over a big glass bowl. As I turn the handle, the cores, seeds, and peelings stay in the top and pink applesauce squirts out of the holes.

"Let's scoop out servings of the warm sauce, one for you and one for me," says Grandma. "I want you to have the very first taste of our special treat."

Healthy Choices

*True or false: a scoop of applesauce
is a healthy food choice?*

If you answered true, you are right! Applesauce, made from apples, fits into the **Fruit** food group. Add the others: **Vegetable**, **Grain**, **Dairy**, and **Meat** and you'll have the Five Food Groups. Can you remember each of these groups? Perhaps this silly sentence will help. **V**ery **g**oofy **d**ogs **f**ollow **m**e. Now remember to choose and eat a variety of nutritious foods from each of these groups each and every day!

Summer Vacation Postcards
Vacation at Lake Erie

Dear Joey, We just reached Geneva-on-the-Lake and Nana's summer cottage. After lunch, we'll walk down the wooden steps to the beach. Nana has four black rubber tubes from huge truck tires. They float in the water. One tube is big enough for my sister and me to share. We sit on it and let the waves splash us to shore. Our dog, Boots, likes the waves, too.

Washin' Ashore, Marcia

Dear Joey, Last night I rode the blue painted boat at the amusement park ride in town. The park's not as big as Cedar Point, but it twinkles with bright lights and has a dance band for grown-ups. We can hear the music from the rides. Later we walked uptown. We heard the park music all through town. We ate French fries on a bench and watched all the people. Tomorrow we are going to Ashtabula with Papa. I hope the bridge will be lifting for the big boats.

Ahoy Matey, Marcia

Dear Joey, Nana pulled off the road at a fruit stand. We helped her carry six quarts of raspberries for jam and a bag of peaches for a pie. We're watching her cook the jam. It is very hot, but it makes the cottage smell like fresh-picked berries. "I'll bake the pie while you swim. We'll have it with vanilla ice cream for dessert tonight," she promises. We took peanut butter and raspberry jam sandwiches down to the beach for a picnic. When we returned, Nana played cards with us on the big picnic table. She is teaching us how to play Canasta. It's a game played with two decks of cards at the same time.

Shuffle, shuffle, Marcia

An Ohio Timeline

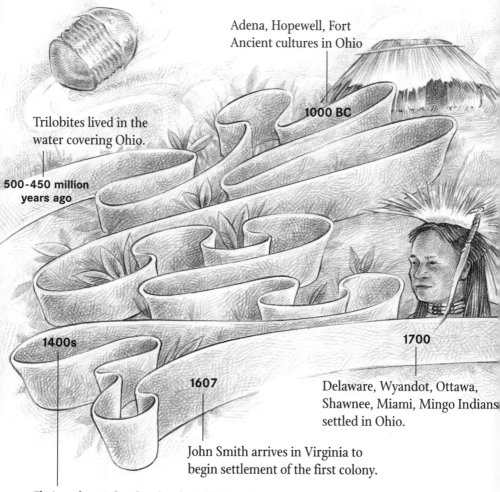

Adena, Hopewell, Fort
Ancient cultures in Ohio

Trilobites lived in the
water covering Ohio.

1000 BC

**500-450 million
years ago**

1400s

1700

1607

Delaware, Wyandot, Ottawa,
Shawnee, Miami, Mingo Indians
settled in Ohio.

John Smith arrives in Virginia to
begin settlement of the first colony.

Christopher Columbus lands in Haiti and
Johannes Gutenburg invents the printing press.

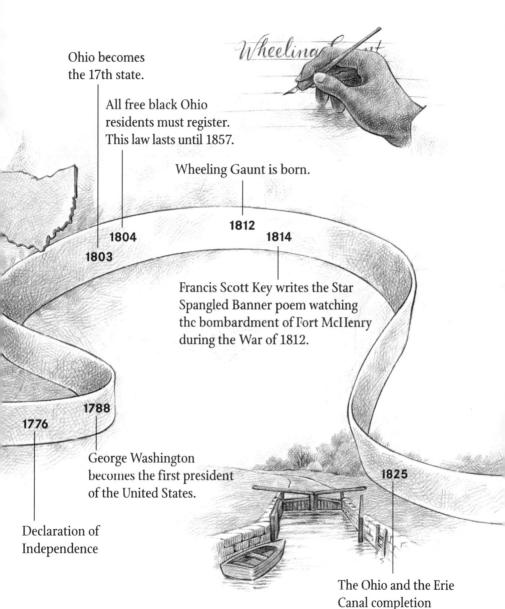

Ohio becomes
the 17th state.

All free black Ohio
residents must register.
This law lasts until 1857.

Wheeling Gaunt is born.

Wheeling Gaunt

1812

1804

1814

1803

Francis Scott Key writes the Star
Spangled Banner poem watching
the bombardment of Fort McHenry
during the War of 1812.

1788

1776

George Washington
becomes the first president
of the United States.

1825

Declaration of
Independence

The Ohio and the Erie
Canal completion

27

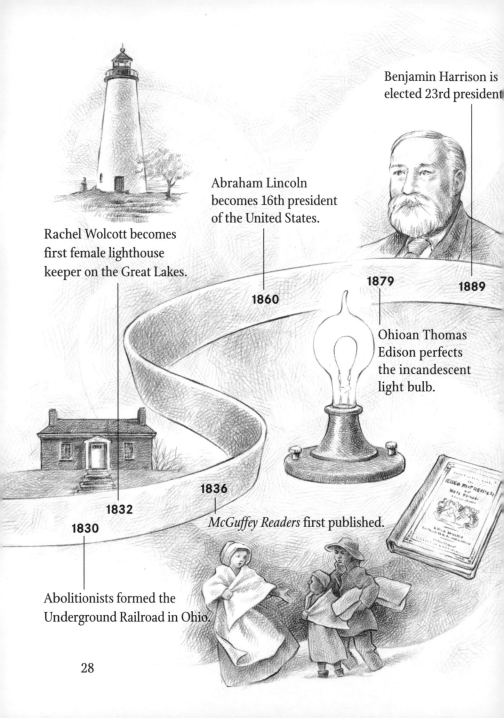

Benjamin Harrison is elected 23rd president

Abraham Lincoln becomes 16th president of the United States.

Rachel Wolcott becomes first female lighthouse keeper on the Great Lakes.

1879

1889

1860

Ohioan Thomas Edison perfects the incandescent light bulb.

1836

1832

1830

McGuffey Readers first published.

Abolitionists formed the Underground Railroad in Ohio.

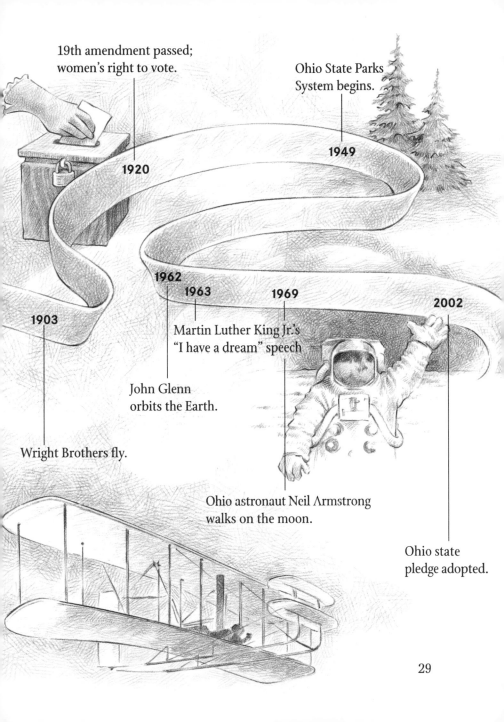

19th amendment passed; women's right to vote.

Ohio State Parks System begins.

1949

1920

1962

1963

1969

2002

1903

Martin Luther King Jr.'s "I have a dream" speech

John Glenn orbits the Earth.

Wright Brothers fly.

Ohio astronaut Neil Armstrong walks on the moon.

Ohio state pledge adopted.

An Ohio Riddle

What has 17 arrows
Without any bows?

A field of wheat
In seventeen rows?

With a bright yellow sun
Rising above the mountain below?

Do you need one more clue?
A blue river flows across it, too.

vocabulary: Adena / draft / constitution / rays / recreation

The Great Seal of Ohio
hides history of our state

Q: *Why are there 13 rays around the sun?*

A: The rays remind us of the 13 original colonies. They rebelled against Great Britain during the American Revolution.

Q: *Why are there 17 rows of wheat and 17 arrows?*

A: The rows represent Ohio as the 17th state and the arrows remind us of the American Indians who were here first. Wheat is symbolic of our agriculture.

Q: *What does the blue river represent?*

A: The Scioto River flows across the seal. In Ohio, it flows from Auglaize County, through Columbus to Portsmouth. It provides drinking water and river recreation before emptying into the Ohio River.

Q: *Where is the real mountain scene represented on the seal?*

A: The sun rising above Mount Logan and the Scioto River Valley looks as it did one early morning from Adena, the Chillicothe mansion of Thomas Worthington. As one of Ohio's founders, Worthington helped draft Ohio's state constitution. In 1814 he became Ohio's sixth governor.

One Clue at a Time

Make a guess when you know.

1. It is not a rectangle, triangle, or square.

2. It has no red, yellow, or blue, but green on its shell.

3. It is seen in the fall, but not for long.

4. It fits in a pocket or in your hand.

5. It is shiny and smooth with one light spot.

Answers: A Buckeye

Here a Chick, There a Chick
So many chickens—thanks to an Ohioan

More than a century ago, before Ohioans drove cars or used electricity, a young boy named Michael Uhl spent his free time helping out on the family farm. After watching over the hens in the chicken coop, his curiosity about how eggs hatched got the best of him.

He carefully observed one of his father's prize hens. He watched her build her nest in the corner of a rail fence. He watched as she strutted through the morning dew before returning to her eggs. He watched as she turned each egg in the nest.

He wrote down what he saw.

1. The hen's wet feet created moist heat.
2. She kept the eggs warm with heat from her body.

He placed a thermometer nearby to record the temperature of the nest. He learned more about humidity.

Soon his quiet observations and detailed notes paid off. At the young age of 14, Michael invented the first incubator for hatching chicks. The year was 1885. The place was New Washington in Crawford County. His incubator held 200 eggs. Heat from oil lamps provided the warmth needed for the eggs to hatch.

Michael stuck to his interest in hatching baby chicks. In 1900 he "hatched" a new industry: shipping baby chicks to other farmers along the railroad that ran through New Washington.

You might know the word *incubator*. An incubator provides a heated environment for hatching eggs. Farmers who raise chickens have been using improved versions of Michael's equipment for more than 100 years.

Trillium

There's a little woodland park
Where we can share a walk.
We'll look for leaves and shallow streams
And have a little talk.

We'll hunt for trillium
Covering the woodland floor.
As soon as we spot one,
We'll likely see some more.

Three white petals
Make triangles against the green.
This lovely Ohio wildflower
Is the prettiest I have seen!

The Youngest Soldier
in the Union Army

CHAPTER ONE

Young Gib Enlists

Soaked and chilled to their bones, the soldiers of the 79th Ohio Volunteer Infantry, Company "D" to be exact, marched on— with the spirit of a bright sunny day. The men, some of whom were really boys, trained together at Camp Dennison, just north of Cincinnati. They marched to the drum beat of young "Gib," short for Gilbert. His given name, Gilbert Van Zandt, sounded too long for such a small soldier. Gib, who was short for his age anyway, looked like he was dressing up, but his costume was authentic. At age ten, he was the youngest soldier in the Union Army of the North.

When Lieutenant Elwood reached Port William to ask for volunteers for President Lincoln's army, Gib begged to drum. Gib's mother hand-stitched navy blue wool into a miniature-sized Union dress uniform that fit Gib perfectly. She added a side stripe on his trousers and purchased a Union kepi, the hat enlistees wore. Children often entertained to help the recruiters attract crowds as they traveled throughout the county.

President Lincoln called for 300,000 enlistees from Ohio and it was Lieutenant Elwood's job to sign up as many soldiers as possible. He paid Gib fifty cents for his help. It was the first money Gib ever earned. His talent as a drummer attracted many enlistees, including his father, uncles, and teacher. Young Gib cried to leave with them. He cried to go on to Camp Dennison,

near Cincinnati, and continue his drum-ming. Never thinking that such a small boy would ever see battle, Gib's parents gave permission. "He'll come back home when the company leaves for battle—or sooner, when he becomes homesick," his mother thought.

Gib did not get homesick. At age ten years, seven months, and 16 days, exactly, Gib enlisted for three years, just like older soldiers. He left his mother, his little brother, and sister. He left his soft bed and his mother's cooking. He left his school friends. He left to become a drummer in Company D. He left to drum in battle.

"How proud I felt with my little drum on my back a-going in the army as a drum-mer boy, and be with the brave soldiers who had started to defend our country," he said.

CHAPTER TWO
A Pony Called Fannie

The soldiers moved on foot and horse-back all the way to Georgia. There they found themselves in the Battle of Resaca in Georgia. During the fighting, the soldiers captured a pony. Since Gib stood only four feet tall—too small for the company's regular horses—he took charge of the pony. He called the pony Fannie Lee. Fannie Lee carried Gib when he couldn't keep up with the steps of grown soldiers.

With Fannie Lee's help, Gib's army job changed from drummer boy to courier. A courier delivers messages, often from the troops' commander to soldiers in the field. It was dangerous work, but Gib acted bravely and courageously. When his captain called for a dispatch bearer to run a hazardous mission, Gib rode up on Fannie Lee.

"You're too small—better go back and send a man," yelled Captain Speed.

"I can do the job, sir," young Gib begged. "Give me the message and let me deliver it." Gib took the message and returned with a receipt late in the night.

Young Gib rode Fannie Lee during famous battles of the Civil War. They rode through the South with General Sherman. They watched the fires in Atlanta. They galloped with General Sherman on his famous march to the sea.

CHAPTER THREE

Gib Goes Home

He and Fannie Lee served until the Civil War ended. After President Lincoln was assassinated, Andrew Johnson became the new president. And Gilbert Van Zandt rode Fannie Lee in the Presidential Review, an official parade of the Union soldiers in Washington, D.C. Gib knew it might be his and Fannie Lee's last ride. She belonged to the government. He would have to give her up.

After the parade, Gib met President Johnson. President Johnson heard about Gib's bravery and his young age. "Would you like to keep Fannie Lee or would you like to become an officer in the Army?" the president asked Gib.

"I'll keep Fannie Lee," exclaimed Gib. With his army discharge papers, young Gib and Fannie Lee left together on the train from Washington to Ohio.

Young Gib, as he was called, was the youngest soldier in the Union Army. He came back to Ohio, but he did not brag about his Civil War career for several reasons. First, Gilbert was a quiet, modest person. Second, his record as the youngest soldier wasn't made public until years after the war when records of enlisted were compared.

Later he moved to Kansas, where he lived until the age of 92. Gilbert Van Zandt became one of the oldest veterans of the Civil War, too.

Mr. Meant-to

The following poem, written many years ago by an anonymous poet, tells the story of what happens when we don't do what we can.

Mr. Meant-to has a comrade,
And his name is Didn't-do;
Have you ever chanced to meet them?
Did they ever call on you?

These two fellows live together
In the house of Never-win,
And I'm told that it is haunted,
By the ghost of Might-have-been.

Doing what we can—helping others, making changes, being on time—involve virtues. A virtue is a good or positive characteristic.

Today students use textbooks, one for each subject. In schools long ago, children often used just one book, called a *McGuffey Eclectic Reader*. The author, William McGuffey, taught college students at Miami University in Oxford, Ohio. He loved children—he had five of his own—and wrote his books for primary grade children. Nearly all U.S. students between 1836 and 1900 learned from his books. The books looked a little like this *Ohio Reader* and included step-by-step lessons on educational topics including reading, animals, and spelling. Many of Professor McGuffey's stories stressed virtues.

Politeness	I would like another cookie, please.
Honesty	I broke the vase.
Kindness	How are you feeling?
Helpfulness	I'll set the table.
Respectfulness	Before taking the first handful, I say, "Would you like some popcorn, Grandpa?"

vocabulary: abolitionists / generosity
Underground Railroad / tolerance

Kindness in a Flour Sack

In 1812 Wheeling Gaunt was born on a tobacco plantation in northern Kentucky. Four years later the plantation master sold Wheeling's mother. Wheeling never saw her again. He began to work as a slave for his master. Somehow he also kept the hope that one day he would change his life.

It would take Wheeling 32 years to save $900—enough money to buy himself from his master. How did he earn the money? He polished shoes, peddled apples, and probably found other odd jobs after working hard on the plantation. Gladly and proudly, he paid for his freedom.

As a free black man, he earned money more quickly—enough to pay for the freedom of two others and even buy some land. Wheeling was free, but not respected because his ancestors came to America as slaves.

Moving to Ohio

Wheeling heard of a small town in Ohio named Yellow Springs. Yellow Springs was a stop on the Underground Railroad. People there were abolitionists and practiced racial tolerance. Other freed slaves lived in Yellow Springs and Wheeling and his family moved there, too.

In Yellow Springs, Wheeling continued buying land. He also worked to improve education and his community. People respected Wheeling and his many virtues, but they did not learn about his true generosity until he died.

A Gift for Generations

When Wheeling Gaunt became ill and elderly, he decided to give nine acres of his land to the town for a special purpose. He instructed officials to use earnings from the property to help others. He wanted to give every poor and worthy widow a bag of flour on Christmas Eve. It would help them through the long, cold winter, he thought. In 1894, the year he died, the widows received 69 sacks of flour.

Now, more than 100 years later, each widow in Yellow Springs receives two gifts from Wheeling Gaunt: a bag of flour and a bag of sugar. These gifts represent the generosity and kindness Wheeling Gaunt continues to teach each new generation who grows up in Yellow Springs.

The Bald Eagle

I see a nest perched high above
In the boughs of a lakeside tree.
Who soars to reach this lofty home?
The proud bald eagle and his family.

The bald eagle, also known as the American Eagle, became a symbol of the United States in 1782. It stands for courage, strength, power, and freedom. If the bald eagle could talk, it would tell a sad story with a happy ending.

The huge bald eagle, with a wingspan of six to eight feet, began losing its freedom as the United States grew from early settlement days. People cut down trees to build cities, factories, and roads. The bald eagle lost its habitat. Then poisonous pesticides and factory waste flowed into rivers and lakes. The eagles, like other plants and animals in the food chain, died. Often birds were hunted for their beautiful feathers and for sport.

Scientists feared the extinction of the bald eagle. They asked legislators to pass laws protecting the American Eagle and other wildlife. The Bald Eagle Protection Act protects our national bird. Even with this law, in place since 1940, the bald eagle was placed on the Endangered Species List in 1967. The situation was serious. There were only four pairs of bald eagles left in Ohio by 1979.

Government workers and citizens worked to save the bald eagle. They passed laws against using certain pesticides and hunting. Other laws protect habitats. Now there are more than 100 nesting bald eagles in our state and thousands throughout the United States. They live in each state except Hawaii, mostly near open water—along sea and lakeshores with tall trees for their heavy nests. Florida is the bald eagle's favorite state, but the nest thought to be the largest was found in Ohio. It was the size of a pickup truck and weighed about two tons.

Here are more interesting facts about our majestic bird:

1. The bald eagle is not really bald. It has white feathers on its head. An Old English word, balde, means white. That is how the American Eagle got its name.

2. The bald eagle can fly up to 40 miles per hour and at heights of 10,000 feet.

3. Bald eagles mate for life and return to the same nest each year.

4. Eagle nests are called *aeries* or *eyries*.

Some Ohio Symbols

Among all state flags, Ohio's is unique.

No other state flies a flag similar to Ohio's. Burgee and swallowtail are two other words for its pennant shape. There are many symbols on our flag, including 17 stars representing Ohio as the 17th state to enter the Union, and the points on the end of the flag in honor of the many hills and valleys of Ohio's landscape.

Look near the woodland ground for these milky white or soft pink blossoms.

Trillium grandiflorum, the botanical name for the Ohio state wildflower, blooms each spring and summer in each of the 88 counties. Because they appear about the same time as robins in spring, they are also called "wake-robins." The word *trillium* comes from the Latin word, meaning three. The trillium has three leaves and three petals.

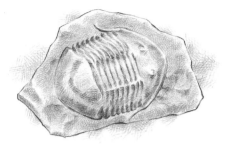

About 500 million years ago a sea creature called a trilobite lived where Ohio is today.

Fossil collectors love the trilobite, a pre-historic insect. A certain one from the Ordovician Period, named Osotelus, is Ohio's most famous—it's the state inver-tebrate fossil. It looked like the horseshoe crabs we see today. Finding a complete trilobite fossil is quite rare; fragments or parts of the insect are more common. The Osotelus is one of the largest trilobites. Some fossils have measured more than 18 inches long!

What are people who live in Ohio called? If you're not from Ohio, it might sound silly to be called a "buckeye," named after the nut on the Ohio Buckeye tree. The nut looks like the eye of a deer. Not only is "buckeye" the nickname for the state, but for residents of Ohio, too. Ohioans have been calling themselves Buckeyes since William Henry Harrison, from Ohio, ran for U.S. president in 1840. His campaign souvenirs were carved from Buckeye tree wood.

More Ohio Symbols

Cardinal
state bird

Flint
state gem

Ladybird Beetle (ladybug)
state insect

White-tailed deer
state animal

Black racer snake
state reptile

Red carnation
state flower

Elijah Pierce
and His Pocketknife

Elijah Pierce already knew how to make wood carvings when he came to Ohio. He learned how to handle a pocketknife before he was seven years old. His uncle taught him how to look for the best carving wood and how to shape little animals. Carving became his favorite hobby. He liked finding wood logs and branches on the woodland floor while his brothers and father tended the family cotton farm in Mississippi.

No one paid much attention to his talent until he grew up. He moved to Columbus, Ohio, and bought his own barber shop. Sometimes, between customers, he'd create tiny animals from wood. Customers thought it was like magic—the way Elijah could turn a wood scrap into something that looked so real.

Once he created a gift for his wife, Cornelia. She loved the miniature elephant. Cornelia put it on a chain and wore it as a necklace. Then Elijah carved a whole zoo of animals for her.

Elijah continued carving, using people from his African-American heritage as models. Some were famous, such as Joe Louis who was a world champion boxer. Others were ordinary people like himself.

He used sandpaper and a few other simple tools. He painted and polished his figures.

Elijah was also a preacher. He enjoyed making characters that told Bible stories and lessons he preached.

Sometimes he gave his miniature sculptures away in exchange for carving wood. Sometimes he sold them at fairs. Elijah

never wondered how his hands, his heart, and his brain managed to make such unique art—all without ever taking an art class. One day, when Elijah was about 78 years old, he entered some of his pieces in a Columbus hobby show. He became a famous artist.

His life changed when sculptors from Ohio State University saw the show. They called him a "folk artist" and showed his work to other artists. Even the Museum of Modern Art in New York City wanted to display his art. He won medals and awards for his sculptures at the age of 80.

Elijah Pierce lived until age 92. His carvings are on display in Ohio at the Martin Luther King Action Center in Columbus and the Columbus Museum of Art.

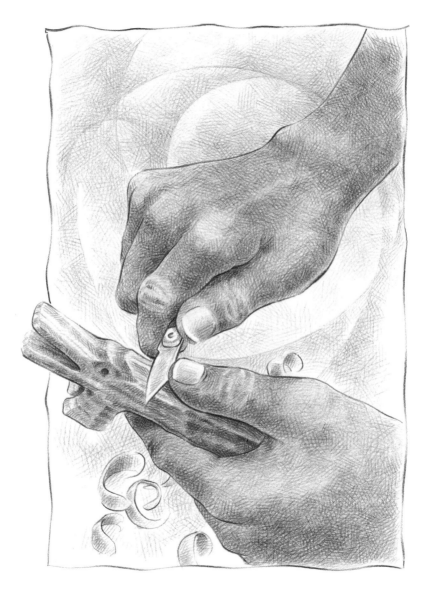

Knife Safety

A pocketknife is a small knife with one or more blades that fold into the handle. It is small enough to fit in a pocket, but like any other knife or sharp object, it is important to handle it safely. Here are two reminder lists:

Do List:

- **Do** fold the blade with the palm of your hand, keeping fingers away from the blade.
- **Do** keep a safe distance from others when using a pocketknife.
- **Do** cut away from the body and body parts.

Do Not List:

- **Do not** take your pocketknife to school or when you are traveling on an airplane.
- To protect nature, **do not** carve or remove bark from trees.
- **Do not** run with an open knife.
- **Do not** throw a knife or keep it open when it isn't being used.

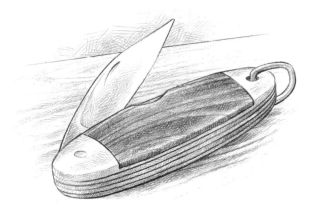

Meeting More Ohio Artists

Many famous artists grew up in Ohio. Their paintings hang in Ohio galleries and all over the United States.

Archibald Willard (1836 – 1918) grew up in Wellington, Ohio. He taught himself how to draw and sketched many scenes while serving in the Civil War. One of his drawings became the idea for his famous painting, *The Spirit of '76*. He called it *Yankee Doodle*, originally.

George Bellows (1892 – 1919) is one of Ohio's most famous painters. He played baseball and took art classes at Ohio State University. He left OSU for New York City to paint with other artists. One of his teachers, Robert Henri, encouraged him to paint scenes of poor, everyday city life. He painted quickly with dark colors. He belonged to a group of painters called the Ashcan School.

Howard Chandler Christy (1873 – 1952) painted many different subjects. Early in his career he illustrated books and magazine articles. He painted bright posters to help the government during World War I. He painted portraits of presidents and other famous people. His most famous painting, *Scene of the Signing of the Constitution of the United States*, hangs in the Capitol in Washington, D.C. The Ohio Statehouse

Rotunda displays his picture of the *Signing of the Treaty of Green Ville.*

Christy was born in Duncan Falls, Ohio. Each summer Morgan County remembers the artist with an outdoor art show.

Frank Duveneck (1848-1919) grew up in Cincinnati, but he was born across the Ohio River in Covington, Kentucky. He studied art at the Royal Academy in Germany and often painted portraits with thick brushstrokes and dark backgrounds. This style is similar to the artists he learned about in Munich. Duveneck lived, painted, and taught art in Cincinnati, but he is well-known throughout the world.

Alice Schille (1869 – 1955) loved to paint. She graduated from art school in Columbus and traveled all over the world to study and make art. She was a plein-air painter, an artist that makes pictures outdoors. Taking watercolors with her, she painted the colorful scenes she saw outside. When she created portraits indoors, she used oil paints. Her style of painting is called Post-Impressionism, but she experimented with other styles, too.

These artists all lived during the same time, but they each expressed different ideas through painting. By studying their lives and painting styles, you can learn more about what happened in Ohio and across the globe during their careers.

Who's an Optimist?

ŏp′tə-mĭst: *one who usually expects a favorable outcome.*

An optimist is happy,
Trying to be glad.
An optimist helps others
By never getting mad.

An optimist thinks ahead,
Forgetting what has passed.
Then on to win the race
To never finish last.

With every mistake,
An optimist would say,
"Improve yourself,
Don't criticize today."

Show friends they're extra special—
Be kind in word and deed.
It's the optimist's way
To feel good and succeed.

Marcia Schonberg

Author Marcia Schonberg combines her love of writing, learning, and teaching in *The Ohio Reader*. Her other very successful books include *B is for Buckeye: An Ohio Alphabet*, *Cardinal Numbers: An Ohio Number Book*, and *I is for Idea: An Inventions Alphabet*. When she writes, she's doing what she knows best and enjoys most—connecting readers with nature, history, and the world around them. Here, Marcia draws from the original *McGuffey Readers* of the nineteenth century [whose author also happens to be from Ohio] to introduce readers to history, symbols and lore of this state. She is also the author of *Ohio Travel Smart* and *Quick Escapes: Cleveland*, and contributes features and photos to magazines and daily newspapers. She lives in Lexington, Ohio with her husband, Bill, and Golden Retriever, Cassie, when she isn't researching Ohio and other fun places to visit.

K.L. Darnell

K.L. Darnell earned her BFA studying drawing and painting at the University of Michigan School of Art and Design. *The Ohio Reader* is Ms. Darnell's sixth children's book with Sleeping Bear Press. In addition to her work as an illustrator, she specializes in the beautiful art of calligraphy and is an instructor of art at Lansing Community College. Ms. Darnell lives in Michigan.